A CITY THROUGH TIME

ILLUSTRATED BY STEVE NOON
WRITTEN BY PHILIP STEELE

CONTENTS

LONDON, NEW YORK, MELBOURNE,
MUNICH AND DELHI

Project Editor Simon Holland
Managing Art Editor Diane Thistlethwaite
Managing Editor Camilla Hallinan
US Editor Margaret Parrish
Production Erica Rosen
Jacket Design Katy Wall
Art Director Simon Webb
Category Publisher Sue Grabham

Additional Illustrators Inklink
and Kevin Jones Associates
Consultants Dr. Hugh Bowden, Professor Anne
Duggan, Dr. Alastair Owens and Philip Wilkinson

First American Edition, 2004

Published in the United States by DK Publishing, Inc.
375 Hudson Street, New York, New York 10014

04 05 06 07 08 09 10 9 8 7 6 5 4 3 2 1

Copyright © 2004 Dorling Kindersley Limited

Published in Great Britain by Dorling Kindersley Limited.

A Cataloging-in-Publication record for this book
is available from the Library of Congress.

ISBN 0-7566-0641-1

Color reproduction by Colourscan, Singapore
Printed and bound in Malaysia by Tien Wah

Discover more at
www.dk.com

THE STORY OF A CITY

Imagine a huge city. Its buildings light up the night sky. Beyond the city center are factories and highways, airports and docks. Tall cranes rise into the sky. Sometimes workers dig up ancient remains, such as Stone Age arrowheads or Roman coins. These show that people have lived here for thousands of years. Some very old buildings still stand. The cathedral has loomed above the rooftops since medieval times.

STONE AGE HUNTERS
(AROUND 14,000 YEARS AGO)

A roaming band of hunters spend each winter on the hill. They sleep in caves and paint pictures on rocks. They fish in the river and collect shellfish on the beach. They make weapons of sharp flints and hardwood. They wear cloaks of animal skin and bone necklaces. Warriors paint their faces with red clay.

A CAMP BY THE RIVER
(AROUND 8,000 YEARS AGO)

Hunters fan out along the river banks. They take careful aim at the ducks. Their arrows are tipped with tiny but deadly flints. The hunters have beached their wooden canoes and set up camp. They have put up tents of deerskin and wooden poles. Soon they will leave and search for new hunting grounds.

Why did people settle here so long ago, at the mouth of a river on the Mediterranean coast? First, there was fresh drinking water. Fish could be caught in the sea. Later, people found that wheat grew well in this soil. There was stone and lumber for building. This was a good place for traders to meet, too. Many sailed here from distant lands. The city grew rich and its rulers became very powerful.

However much the city changed, the people who lived there had the same basic needs as those first settlers. They wanted fresh water, food, and shelter. They wanted to lead healthy and happy lives. They wanted work, trade, and travel by land and sea. They wanted a city that was organized and well run. If we could meet our ancestors, we would probably discover that they were very like ourselves.

THE FIRST FARMERS
(AROUND 6,000 YEARS AGO)

Now there are stone, wooden, and thatch huts on the hillside all year round. This is a farming village. People still hunt, but they no longer need to move in search of food. The harvest gives them enough food for the whole year. The farmers cut the crop with flint sickles.

TOMBS TO HONOR THE DEAD
(AROUND 5,000 YEARS AGO)

Slabs of rock are broken off the cliffs by the river. They are chipped into shape and hauled away with ropes. The chief of the tribe is building an awesome tomb of earth and stone. He will be laid there when he dies. Everyone who sees the tomb will honor his memory.

THE METALWORKERS
(AROUND 4,500 YEARS AGO)

The villagers have learned to mine copper and to separate it from the rock by heat. They pour the molten metal into molds and make it into weapons and jewelry. These can be exchanged with other tribes in return for food and goods.

TRADERS FROM THE SEA
(AROUND 3,000 YEARS AGO)

Merchant ships are drawn up on the beach below the settlement. The sailors are Phoenicians and Cretans, from far to the east. They trade in glass beads, cloth, lumber, and wine from across the sea. Some of these foreign traders settle here.

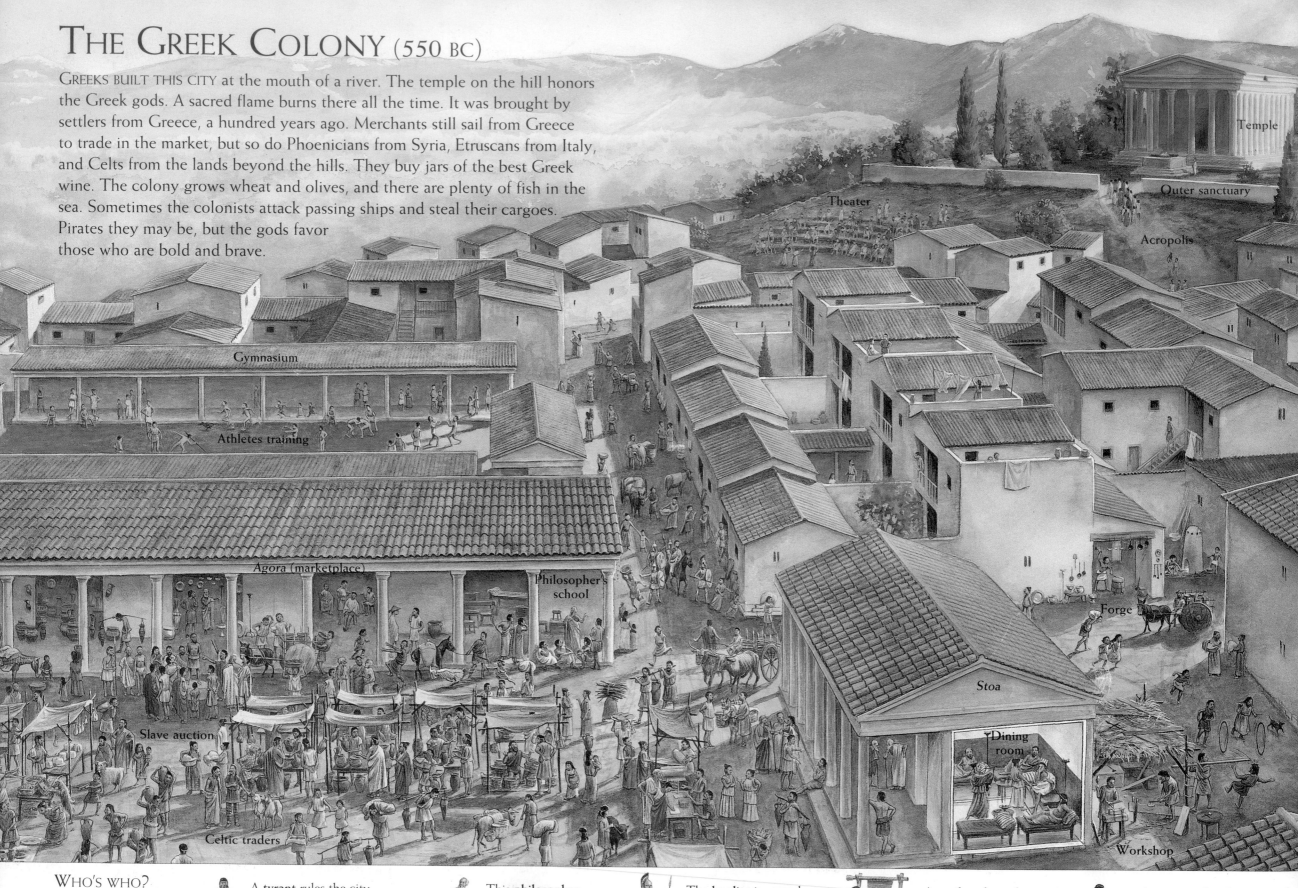

THE GREEK COLONY (550 BC)

GREEKS BUILT THIS CITY at the mouth of a river. The temple on the hill honors the Greek gods. A sacred flame burns there all the time. It was brought by settlers from Greece, a hundred years ago. Merchants still sail from Greece to trade in the market, but so do Phoenicians from Syria, Etruscans from Italy, and Celts from the lands beyond the hills. They buy jars of the best Greek wine. The colony grows wheat and olives, and there are plenty of fish in the sea. Sometimes the colonists attack passing ships and steal their cargoes. Pirates they may be, but the gods favor those who are bold and brave.

Temple

Outer sanctuary

Theater

Acropolis

Gymnasium

Athletes training

Agora (marketplace)

Philosopher's school

Forge

Stoa

Slave auction

Dining room

Celtic traders

Workshop

WHO'S WHO?

Here are some of the people you might meet in the Greek colony.

A **tyrant** rules the city. Descendants of the first settlers despise him because he seeks power and wealth.

This **philosopher** wants to find out why things exist and what they are made of.

The **hoplite** is named after his round shield, the hoplon. He fights with spear and sword.

A **mother** shows her daughters how to weave a woolen blanket on an upright loom.

As soon as they have finished classes with their tutor, the **children** run out to play.

4

Country temple

Threshing

Quarry

Pottery

Landing stage

Olive groves

Wealthy merchant's house

Boatyard

Women's quarters

Classes

Shepherd

Kitchen

Bathroom

Wheat harvest

Household altar

Hoplites

 A **merchant** carries vegetables, leeks, and onions to market on the back of his donkey.

 This **bride** is 18 years old. She is trying on a veil in preparation for her wedding day.

 The **potter** shapes wet clay with his fingers. He makes cups, jugs, storage jars, and bowls.

 This **athlete** is famous. He traveled all the way to Greece for the Olympic Games.

 A **girl** plucks the strings of a lyre. She is playing at a banquet.

 A **fisherman** walks back from the seashore. His catch should fetch a good price at market.

 A **slave** carries water from the well. She was born far to the east, in Thrace.

5

THE TEMPLE (550 BC)

TODAY THERE IS A HARVEST FESTIVAL, to honor the goddess Demeter. An excited procession winds up the hill to the new temple. Everyone looks up at the great marble columns, which soar to the sky. The old temple was made of wood. Oxen bellow as they are led to be killed at the altar. This sacrifice will bring good fortune to the city. The Greeks worship many gods and goddesses. The sailor prays to Poseidon for calm seas. The hunter asks Artemis to guide his spear. Every child knows the old tales about the gods. The stories are exciting, for the gods are always quarreling, playing tricks, or falling in love.

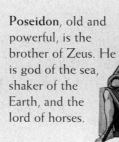

Altar

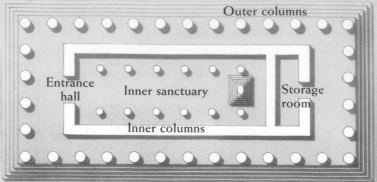

Outer columns

Entrance hall · Inner sanctuary · Storage room

Inner columns

ALTAR AND TEMPLE

Public ceremonies take place at the altar outside the temple. Private worship may take place in the half-light of the inner sanctuary, or holy place, which contains statues and treasure.

TEMPLE DECORATION

Painted stone sculptures decorate the roof. They show scenes of gods, humans, animals, and strange beasts.

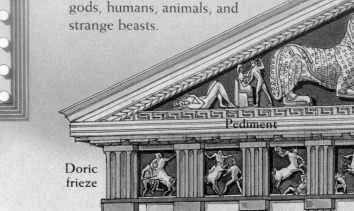

Pediment

Doric frieze

Architrave

Capital

Doric column

Altar

GREEK GODS

Zeus is father of the gods. He rules Earth from Mount Olympus. If angry, he hurls down lightning and thunderbolts.

Athena, daughter of Zeus, is goddess of battle and wisdom. She protects olive groves and many cities in the Greek world.

Artemis, another daughter of Zeus, is the goddess of wild animals and hunting. She is armed with a bow and arrows.

Poseidon, old and powerful, is the brother of Zeus. He is god of the sea, shaker of the Earth, and the lord of horses.

Demeter is goddess of grain, the seasons, fertility, and death. She is worshipped wherever the Greeks have settled.

THE PROCESSION

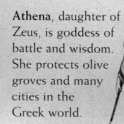

A life-size, painted statue of the grain goddess, Demeter, is hauled through the streets. Some of the people carry sheaves of wheat in her honor. Horses prance and children sing to the music of flutes.

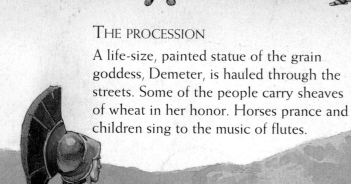

Life-size statue of Demeter

Outer sanctuary of the temple

Ox for sacrifice

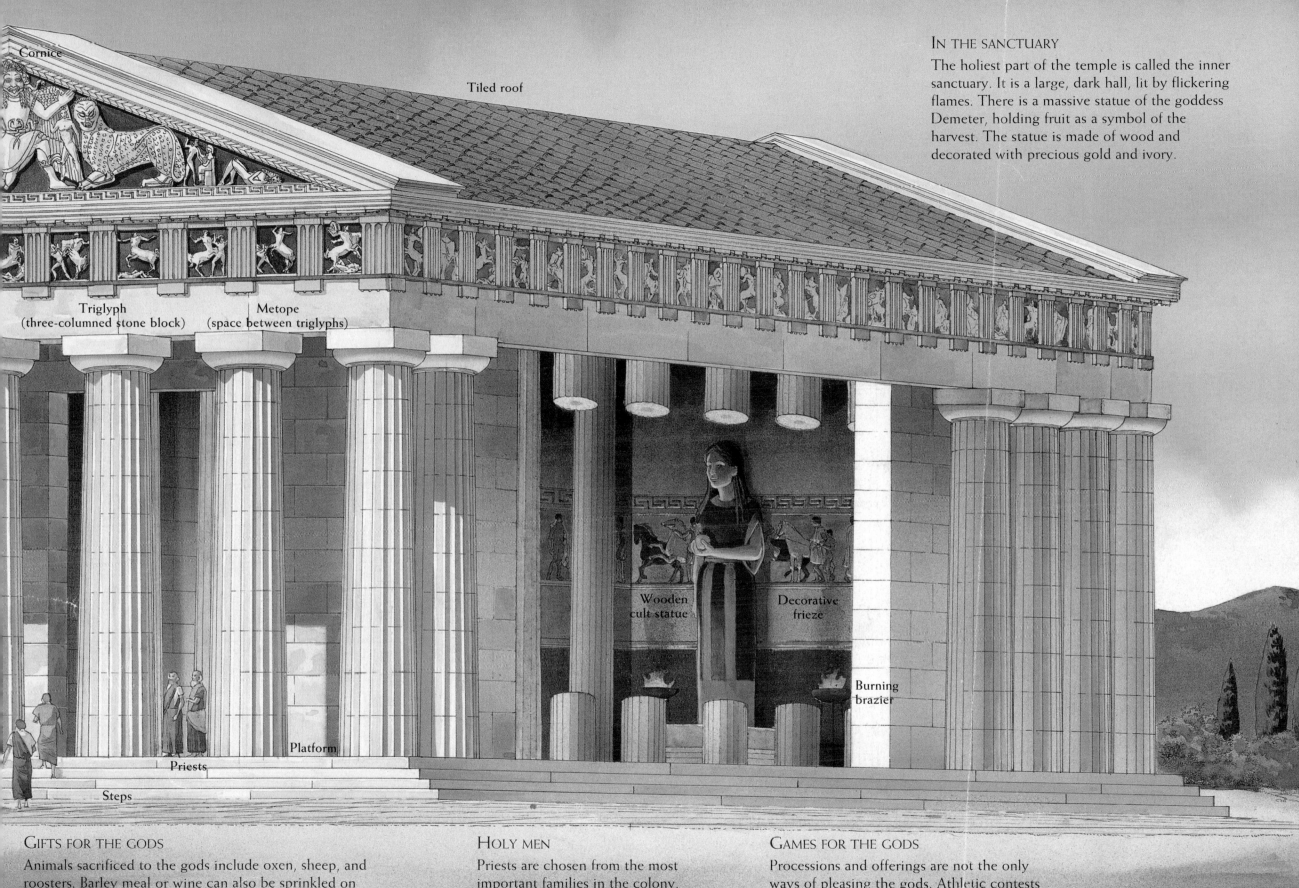

Cornice

Tiled roof

IN THE SANCTUARY

The holiest part of the temple is called the inner sanctuary. It is a large, dark hall, lit by flickering flames. There is a massive statue of the goddess Demeter, holding fruit as a symbol of the harvest. The statue is made of wood and decorated with precious gold and ivory.

Triglyph
(three-columned stone block)

Metope
(space between triglyphs)

Wooden
cult statue

Decorative
frieze

Burning
brazier

Platform

Priests

Steps

GIFTS FOR THE GODS

Animals sacrificed to the gods include oxen, sheep, and roosters. Barley meal or wine can also be sprinkled on the altar. Another way to please the gods is to give money to the temple priests.

HOLY MEN

Priests are chosen from the most important families in the colony. They make sure that all the rituals and ceremonies are followed properly.

GAMES FOR THE GODS

Processions and offerings are not the only ways of pleasing the gods. Athletic contests are also held in their honor. Even in times of war, all fighting ceases during the games.

7

CITIZENS OF ROME (AD 120)

THE STREETS ARE STRAIGHT and paved. Soldiers patrol the city walls. The Romans are now in control of the city. The Roman empire stretches from the Atlantic Ocean in the west to beyond the Black Sea in the east. In addition to most of Europe, it covers parts of North Africa and Asia. Merchants, messengers, and officials arrive in the city from distant lands. They make offerings at the temple on the hill. The Romans worship the same gods as the Greeks, although they call them different names. The visitors dine with leading citizens and relax at the public baths. They are jostled by crowds on their way to the amphitheater. Today a famous gladiator is fighting in the ring.

Theater

Insula (apartment block)

Storehouses

Temple

Basilica (center for law and commerce)

Business center

Law courts

Market

Political speaker

Forum

Apartments

Toilets

Cavalry

Domus (house) of a wealthy merchant

Water fountain

Doctor

Music lesson

Matron

Women's quarters

Patron and clients

Household slave

Shops

Household shrine

Thermopolium (snack bar)

Litter

Atrium (main room)

Political graffiti

Peristylium (courtyard garden)

Patron

Client

Cloth merchant

Litter

Tablinium (office)

Paved street

Stepping-stones

WHO'S WHO?

Here are some of the people you might meet in the Roman city.

This rich **patron** wants to be a politician. He has powerful friends in business and in the courts of law.

The **client** supports the patron's business deals and political schemes. He is given money in return.

Slaves work as servants or laborers. In the end, a lucky few might be given their freedom.

The **legionary** belongs to an army unit called a legion. He might have to serve anywhere in the Roman empire.

This **gladiator** was once a criminal. He was let off so that he could fight in the ring for people's entertainment.

8

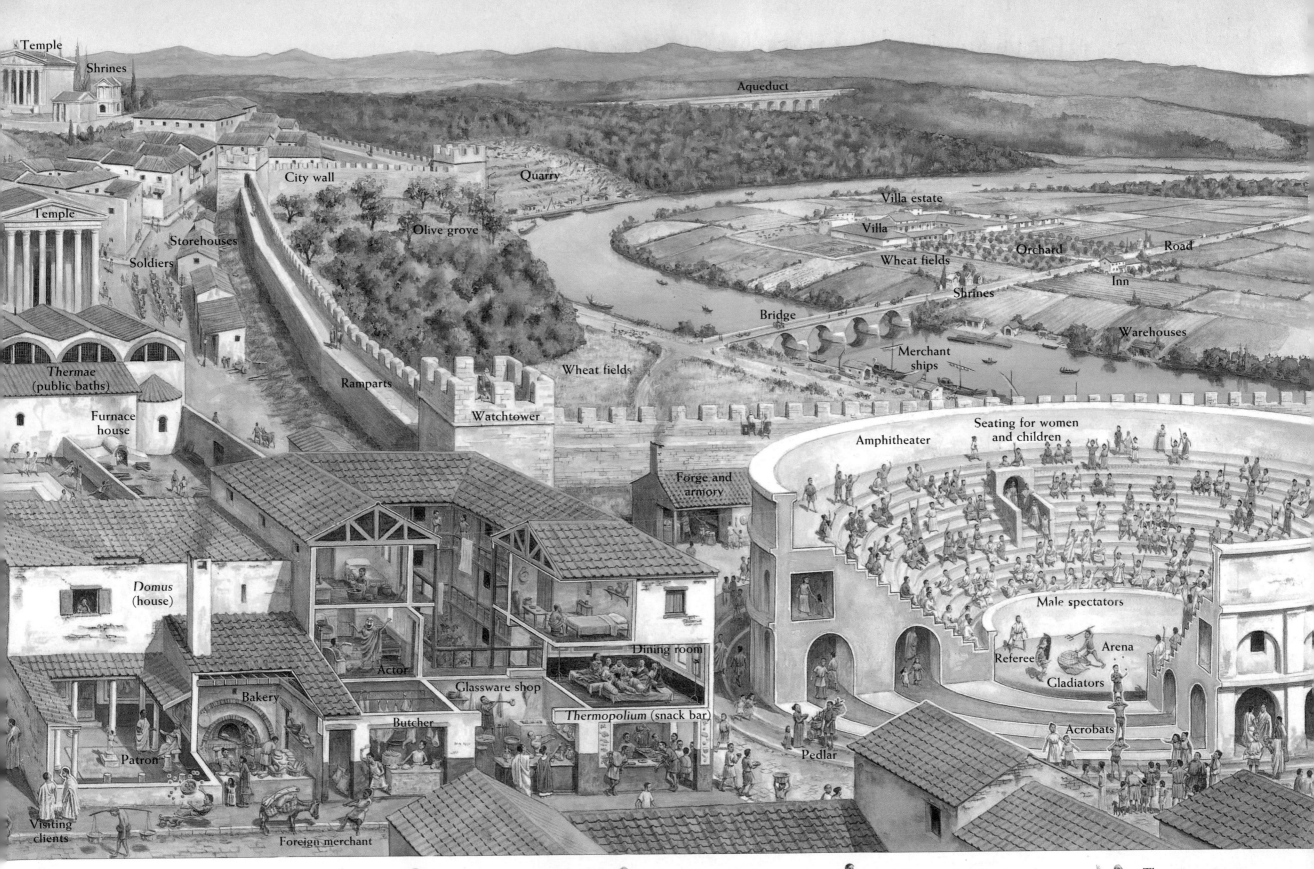

Temple

Shrines

Aqueduct

City wall

Quarry

Temple

Villa estate

Villa

Storehouses

Olive grove

Orchard

Road

Soldiers

Wheat fields

Inn

Shrines

Bridge

Warehouses

Thermae
(public baths)

Wheat fields

Merchant
ships

Ramparts

Furnace
house

Watchtower

Amphitheater

Seating for women
and children

Forge and
armory

Domus
(house)

Male spectators

Referee

Arena

Actor

Dining room

Gladiators

Bakery

Glassware shop

Butcher

Thermopolium (snack bar)

Acrobats

Patron

Pedlar

Visiting
clients

Foreign merchant

 This **laborer** is
employed by the
town council to repair
roads and bridges.

 A **young woman**
practices the cithara,
a musical instrument
first used in Greece.

 This rich **married woman**
has four children. She runs
her own small business,
and rents out some shops.

 An **old man** hurries home
to his little farm outside the
city walls. He has been selling
honey in town.

 A **draper** sells rolls of woolen or
linen cloth. Cotton is sometimes
imported from Egypt. Silk from
Asia is rare and very expensive.

 The **actor** wears a
sad mask for tragedies
and a happy mask
for comedies.

9

THE PUBLIC BATHS (AD 120)

THE BATHHOUSE IS BUSY today. Slaves hurry through the steam, carrying fresh towels. Is it to be the hot room or the cold room? The warm bath or the cold plunge? A massage or a workout? Everyone loves the baths. Businessmen swap stories and mop their brows. Soldiers quarrel and play dice. Tomorrow it is the women's turn. They laugh and chat as they do their sewing. Visiting the baths is part of the Roman way of life.

BATHING IN STYLE
The floors are decorated with mosaics. These are pictures or patterns made out of fragments of colored stone, pottery, or glass.

THE ROUTINE
Slaves clean and massage bathers after their exercise. Bathers can then choose a cold plunge or go straight to the warm room. The hot room offers a relaxing soak in the small pool. Finally, bathers freshen up with a cold dip.

Flue

Vent

Frigidarium (cold room)

Splash basin

Tiled roof

Guttering

Wall paintings

Apodyteria (changing room)

Lockers

Drainpipe

Tepidarium (warm room)

Mosaics

Caldarium (hot room)

Cleaning and oiling

Alveus (bath)

Heated floor

Body massage

Heating ducts

Hypocaust (underground heating)

Furnace

Street gutter

Slave

Toilets

Wrestling

Palaestra (exercise yard)

Weightlifting

Decorative pool

Sprinting

10

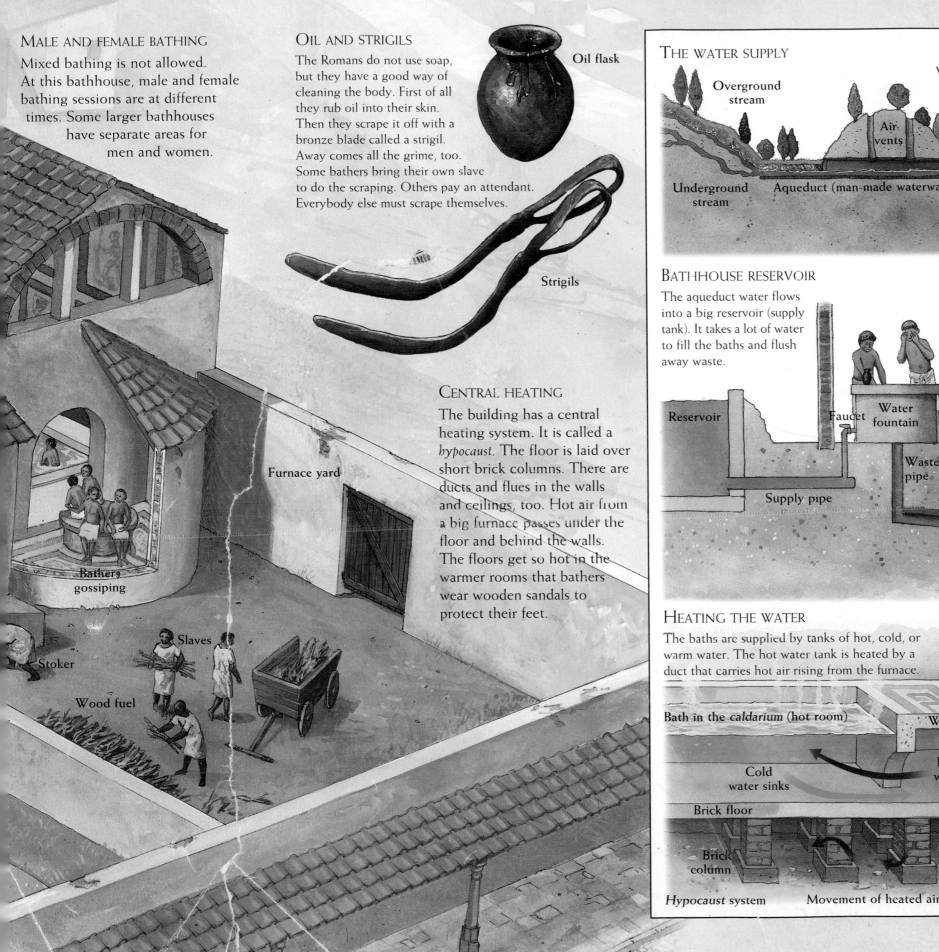

MALE AND FEMALE BATHING

Mixed bathing is not allowed. At this bathhouse, male and female bathing sessions are at different times. Some larger bathhouses have separate areas for men and women.

OIL AND STRIGILS

The Romans do not use soap, but they have a good way of cleaning the body. First of all they rub oil into their skin. Then they scrape it off with a bronze blade called a strigil. Away comes all the grime, too. Some bathers bring their own slave to do the scraping. Others pay an attendant. Everybody else must scrape themselves.

Oil flask

Strigils

CENTRAL HEATING

The building has a central heating system. It is called a *hypocaust*. The floor is laid over short brick columns. There are ducts and flues in the walls and ceilings, too. Hot air from a big furnace passes under the floor and behind the walls. The floors get so hot in the warmer rooms that bathers wear wooden sandals to protect their feet.

Furnace yard

Bathers gossiping

Stoker

Slaves

Wood fuel

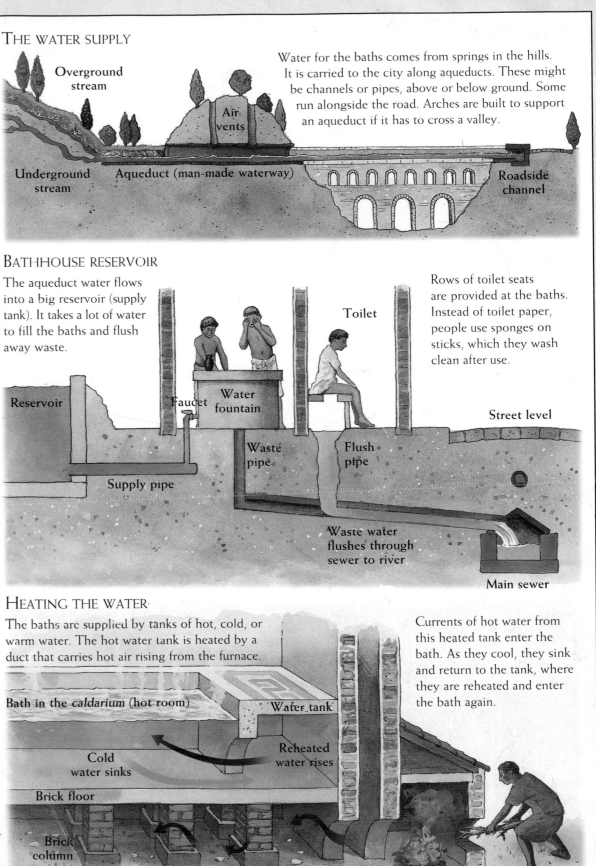

THE WATER SUPPLY

Water for the baths comes from springs in the hills. It is carried to the city along aqueducts. These might be channels or pipes, above or below ground. Some run alongside the road. Arches are built to support an aqueduct if it has to cross a valley.

Overground stream

Air vents

Underground stream

Aqueduct (man-made waterway)

Roadside channel

BATHHOUSE RESERVOIR

The aqueduct water flows into a big reservoir (supply tank). It takes a lot of water to fill the baths and flush away waste.

Rows of toilet seats are provided at the baths. Instead of toilet paper, people use sponges on sticks, which they wash clean after use.

Toilet

Reservoir

Faucet

Water fountain

Street level

Supply pipe

Waste pipe

Flush pipe

Waste water flushes through sewer to river

Main sewer

HEATING THE WATER

The baths are supplied by tanks of hot, cold, or warm water. The hot water tank is heated by a duct that carries hot air rising from the furnace.

Currents of hot water from this heated tank enter the bath. As they cool, they sink and return to the tank, where they are reheated and enter the bath again.

Bath in the *caldarium* (hot room)

Water tank

Cold water sinks

Reheated water rises

Brick floor

Brick column

Hypocaust system

Movement of heated air

Duct

Furnace

THE MEDIEVAL CITY (1250)

IT IS A GRAY WINTER'S day. A massive castle towers over the city and the river. It belongs to the count, one of the most powerful men in the land. A new cathedral is rising above the rooftops, too, a symbol of the Church's power and wealth in these times. The city has been Christian now for over 900 years. Pilgrims come here to pray and knights are blessed by the bishop as they ride off to war. The city streets may be narrow and dirty, but the market square is busy and prosperous. Just look at the fine town hall and merchants' houses.

Cathedral of Our Lady

Builders

Scaffolding

Common land

City watch

Roman ruins

Roman turret

Blacksmith's forge

Tilers

Scribe

Wet nurse

Washerwomen

Spinster

Armorer

Corn merchant

Tailor

WHO'S WHO?

Here are some of the people you might meet in the medieval city.

 The **king** rules over all the land. Even the count must obey him, although they often quarrel.

 The **Pope** is head of the Church in Rome. He is even more powerful than the king.

 The **bishop** is the regional Church leader, and very proud of his splendid new cathedral.

 Monks and nuns follow a life of prayer. Some teach and some care for the sick.

 The **count** governs the whole region. He is very rich. Knights swear loyalty to him.

The count's castle

Roman ruins

Monastery

Monastery fields

Olive grove

City bridge

The count's fields

City wall

Traitors' heads on pikes

East Gate

Town hall

Weight master

Tavern

Iron dealer

Dye factory

Banker

Butcher

Bakery

Cobbler

Poultry stall

Miracle play

Pail stall

Cloth stall

Crusader knights

Countess's carriage

Sheep

Packhorses

Leather goods

Mason with blocks of stone

Pilgrims

Juggler

Pedlar

 This **lawyer** studied at the University of Bologna, in Italy. His dealings have made him wealthy.

 A **blacksmith** shoes horses and mends tools and weapons at his forge. It is thirsty work!

 Merchants buy and sell goods in the marketplace. Some of them make more money than the nobles.

 Foot soldiers are in the service of the knights and the nobles. They guard the count's castle.

 Poor **farmworkers** plow the fields on the count's land. They are not allowed to leave or work for anyone else.

 City workers include builders, carpenters, servants, washerwomen, and sewage shovelers.

THE CASTLE (1250)

TODAY THE COUNT is entertaining noble guests. They shiver as they ride through the gate and look up at the grim towers. Who would ever dare to attack this castle? Its walls extend to surround the whole city. Knights ride out from here to fight the count's enemies. Castle officials ride through the count's lands, collecting taxes. Nobody likes them! City and country folk alike must supply the castle with labor or food.

IN THE GARDEN

The countess likes to walk in the garden. Herbs are grown here to make medicines for the sick or wounded. There are herbs for cooking, too, and sweet-smelling plants that are picked and scattered on the castle floors. Birds of prey are kept in a special enclosure, called the mews. The count and countess like to hunt with falcons.

WHEN WAS THE CASTLE BUILT?

In the 400s, the Roman city came under attack from Germanic warriors. Much of it was burned down. Warrior chiefs split the region into small kingdoms and waged endless wars on each other. Then, in 950, one king conquered the whole region. He appointed a count to rule it in his name. The count built a castle of wood, but that was soon destroyed. In 1070 a great tower was built in stone. Since then, more stone walls and towers have been added to the castle.

SHOOTING ARROWS

There are not many guards on duty today. When the city is under siege, surrounded by the enemy, the walls swarm with soldiers. They clatter up the towers' spiral stairs. When the arrows fly, the soldiers crouch behind merlons. They return fire through the gaps in the walls, called crenels.

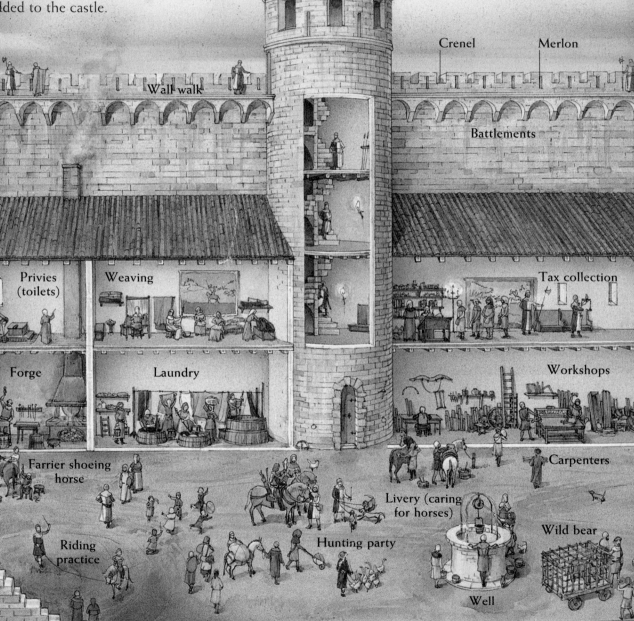
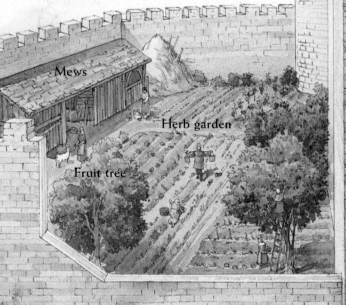

Eagle Tower

North Tower

West Tower

Crenel

Merlon

Battlements

Loop (arrow slit)

Watchmen

Wall walk

Mews

Tax collection

Herb garden

Privies (toilets)

Weaving

Fruit tree

Prison chamber

Forge

Laundry

Workshops

Guard room

Farrier shoeing horse

Carpenters

Livery (caring for horses)

Riding practice

Hunting party

Wild bear

Well

Bailey (courtyard and inner walls)

Chapel
Tower

King's
Tower

River Tower

A NOBLE LIFE

The castle is a home as well as a stronghold.
The count and his family live safely in the
towers. There are less comfortable rooms
for servants and men-at-arms.

Chapel

Guard
room

Ransomed
captive

Kitchens

Bedroom

Solar
(living room)

Great
hall

Buttery
(food
store)

Ladies'
chamber

Banquet

Cellar

Food deliveries

Weapons
training

Inner
Gate

Visiting nobles

BECOMING A KNIGHT

A young boy is chosen from
a wealthy or noble family. He
is sent to work as page in a
nobleman's castle. He works hard
and is taught good manners.

Alongside his daily chores,
the page also learns how to ride
a horse well and how to fight
using practice weapons.

The page becomes a squire
to a knight in the service
of the nobleman. He helps
the knight with his armor
and weapons and prepares
his horse for battle.

The squire soon masters
his own use of weapons
and accompanies the
knight into battle. He
becomes known for
his bravery in action.

After making vows
to God and oaths of
loyalty to his lord, he is
"knighted" by a noble
or by the king himself.

The new knight seeks
glory on the battlefield,
wearing the coat-of-arms
of his family. He also
wants wealth at home.
To succeed, he must
marry well and win
powerful friends.

15

PALACES AND FOUNTAINS (1650)

HOOVES CLATTER AND CART WHEELS RUMBLE over the cobblestones. Street sellers call out their wares: "Come buy!" Around the tavern, a group of rowdy musketeers is singing out of tune. Pickpockets loiter in the alleys. Rats scamper along the wharfs by the river and wriggle through attics and gutters. In the city square, fashionable ladies and gentlemen are bowing and curtseying to each other. The most splendid silks and lace are worn by the count and countess. Their grand palace is built on the hill, beside the ruins of the old castle.

Cathedral

Palace

Castle ruins

Priest attending to the sick

Bed chamber

Market

Artist's studio

Gamblers

Alchemist

Hatter

Pewter goods

Business meeting

Cloth merchant's house

Spice shop

Tailor

Bank

Inn

Apothecary (pharmacist)

Gunsmith

Water seller

Pikemen

Musketeers

Packhorses

WHO'S WHO?
Here are some of the people you might meet in the city in the 17th century.

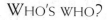

The **count** and **countess** are the city's wealthiest couple. They spend most of their time away at the royal court.

The **footman** is a servant who opens the doors of coaches, ushers in guests, and serves at table.

This **actress** appears in comedies at the theater. She is very popular with everyone in the city.

The **musketeer** is armed with a gun called a musket. He is meant to keep order, but often gets into brawls.

This is the **daughter** of a cloth merchant. She has run off with her brother's hobbyhorse.

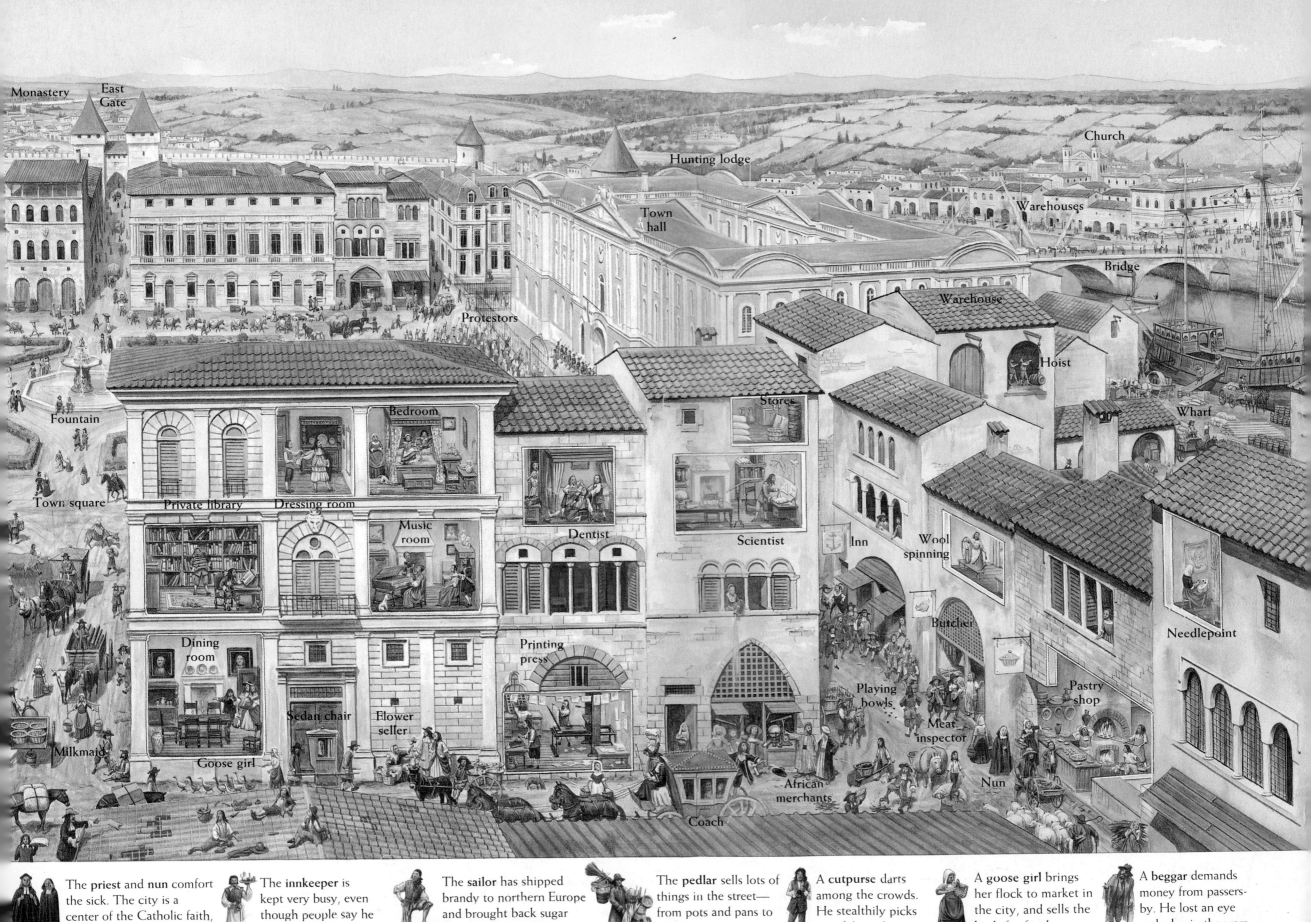

Monastery

East Gate

Hunting lodge

Church

Town hall

Warehouses

Protestors

Bridge

Warehouse

Fountain

Hoist

Bedroom

Stores

Wharf

Town square

Private library

Dressing room

Music room

Dentist

Scientist

Inn

Wool spinning

Dining room

Printing press

Butcher

Needlepoint

Milkmaid

Sedan chair

Flower seller

Playing bowls

Pastry shop

Goose girl

African merchants

Meat inspector

Nun

Coach

The **priest** and **nun** comfort the sick. The city is a center of the Catholic faith, with many new churches.

The **innkeeper** is kept very busy, even though people say he waters down the wine.

The **sailor** has shipped brandy to northern Europe and brought back sugar from the West Indies.

The **pedlar** sells lots of things in the street— from pots and pans to ribbons and toys.

A **cutpurse** darts among the crowds. He stealthily picks people's pockets.

A **goose girl** brings her flock to market in the city, and sells the birds for food.

A **beggar** demands money from passers- by. He lost an eye and a leg in the wars.

17

THE TOWN HALL (1650)

THE HARVEST THIS YEAR was a poor one. Grain is scarce, so flour and bread have become very expensive. Only the rich can afford to buy them. Hungry protestors gather at the gates of the town hall. Their angry cries echo around the courtyard. They want food for their families. Clerks in the tax office drop their quill pens in panic, spilling ink. "Call out the Guard!" bellows one. "Summon the Grand Council!" yells another.

INSIDE THE CITY HALL

The city is run from this grand public building. Tables are piled high with papers and books. Royal officials argue with tax collectors, lawyers, and clerks.

MUSKETEERS AND CANNONBALLS

Infantry carry muskets or pikes. Muskets are guns fired with a small charge of gunpowder. Pikes are pointed spears.

Musket

Sword

Pike

Gunner

Loading shot

Fuse

Cannon

Gun carriage

Cannonballs

Cannon are mounted on the city walls and along the wharfs of the river and harbor. About a hundred years ago, cannon fire knocked down most of the old castle towers.

PREPARING A BANQUET

Members of the Grand Council are already in the building. A banquet is being prepared for them. Servants lay out silver plates. Cooks shout out orders in the steamy kitchen.

POSING FOR A PORTRAIT

The commander of the guard is having his portrait painted. When the trouble starts, he runs downstairs to the guard room, brandishing his sword.

TOO MUCH TAX!

People cannot afford to pay taxes, but the king needs money to pay for his foreign wars. Tax collectors go around the city. They bully people and threaten them with jail.

City coat-of-arms

Guards

Town clock

Emergency meeting

Court of law

Judge

Spectators

Wooden staircase

Gallery

Accused robber

Musketeers

Lockup

Safe

Guard room

Armory

Protestors

MEETING OF THE GRAND COUNCIL

The count's secretary, the bishop, the chief justice, and the master of the guilds all refuse to give in to the mob. A royal official flings open a window. "Go away or we will shoot you down!" he yells. The crowd hesitates, then scatters.

ARM YOURSELVES!

The civil guard carry swords, muskets, and pistols. Weapons are kept in the armory, but gunpowder is kept in the castle ruins because of the risk of fire.

THE COURTROOM

A prisoner stands in the courtroom, accused of highway robbery. Other prisoners are held in the lockup, awaiting trial.

19

THE INDUSTRIAL PORT (1880)

FACTORY CHIMNEYS RISE above the rooftops. Trains clank and hiss at the station, belching out smoke. People close their apartment shutters to block out the heat and noise. Over two million people live here now. The city's suburbs stretch all the way to the new docks at the mouth of the river. There, big ships bring sugar, cotton, hardwoods, coffee, and tea from distant lands. The city's water supply is still poor, but new drains and sewers are being built and there is a new hospital.

Cathedral being restored

Palace

Castle ruins

East Gate

Railroad bridge

Museum

Town hall

Town square

Family apartment

Nursery

Dressing for dinner

Traveling salesman

Hotel

Balcony

Confectioner's

Chimney sweeps

Study

Coffee time

Advertisements

Lamplighter

Cab

Nanny

Jewelers

Needleworkers

Restaurant

Shoe shine

Grocer's shop

Jeweler's shop

Draper's shop

Coffee shop

Street sweeper

Fruit seller

Photographer

Omnibus

Paperboy

Organ grinder

Pie man

Barrow

Flower seller

Coal cart

Vegetable cart

Steam carriage

Milk cart

Velocipede

WHO'S WHO?

Here are some of the people you might meet in the industrial city.

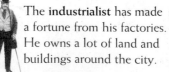 The **industrialist** has made a fortune from his factories. He owns a lot of land and buildings around the city.

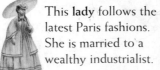 This **lady** follows the latest Paris fashions. She is married to a wealthy industrialist.

 The **soldier** is due to report at the railroad station. He is being sent to serve with troops in an overseas colony.

 The **girl** has been given a fine china doll. It was made in Germany.

The **nanny** wheels a baby carriage. She works for a family that has many children to look after.

 The **grocer** wears a long white apron. His fruit and vegetables are neatly stacked and displayed.

Industrial quarter

Hospital

Botanical gardens

Hot-air balloon

Mills

Prison

Opera house

Railroad station

University

Suspension bridge

Park

Street to the new port

Advertisements

Lumber

Inner city wharves

Coal barge

Paddle steamer

Washing

Brush making

Coopérage (barrel-making)

Cloth hall

Crane

Weaving

Shutters

River polluted by sewage and industrial waste

Barrels of wine

Bales of cloth

Bakery

Dray (sideless wagon)

Fish seller

Textile workshop

Match seller

Wagon

Automated loom

Thief

Policeman

Digging drains

Sailing barge

Knife-sharpener

 The **policeman** wears a neat uniform. He blows his whistle if he spots trouble.

 The **cab driver** knows every street in the city and its growing suburbs. His horse is very well-groomed.

 The **flower seller** sells boutonnieres and posies to brighten up people's clothes and homes.

 The **textile worker** moved to the city to find factory work. Cloth-making is a growing industry.

 The **lamplighter** does his rounds each evening. He must light every gas lamp in the street.

 A **newspaper boy** calls out the latest headline: "Scandal at the town hall! Read all about it!"

21

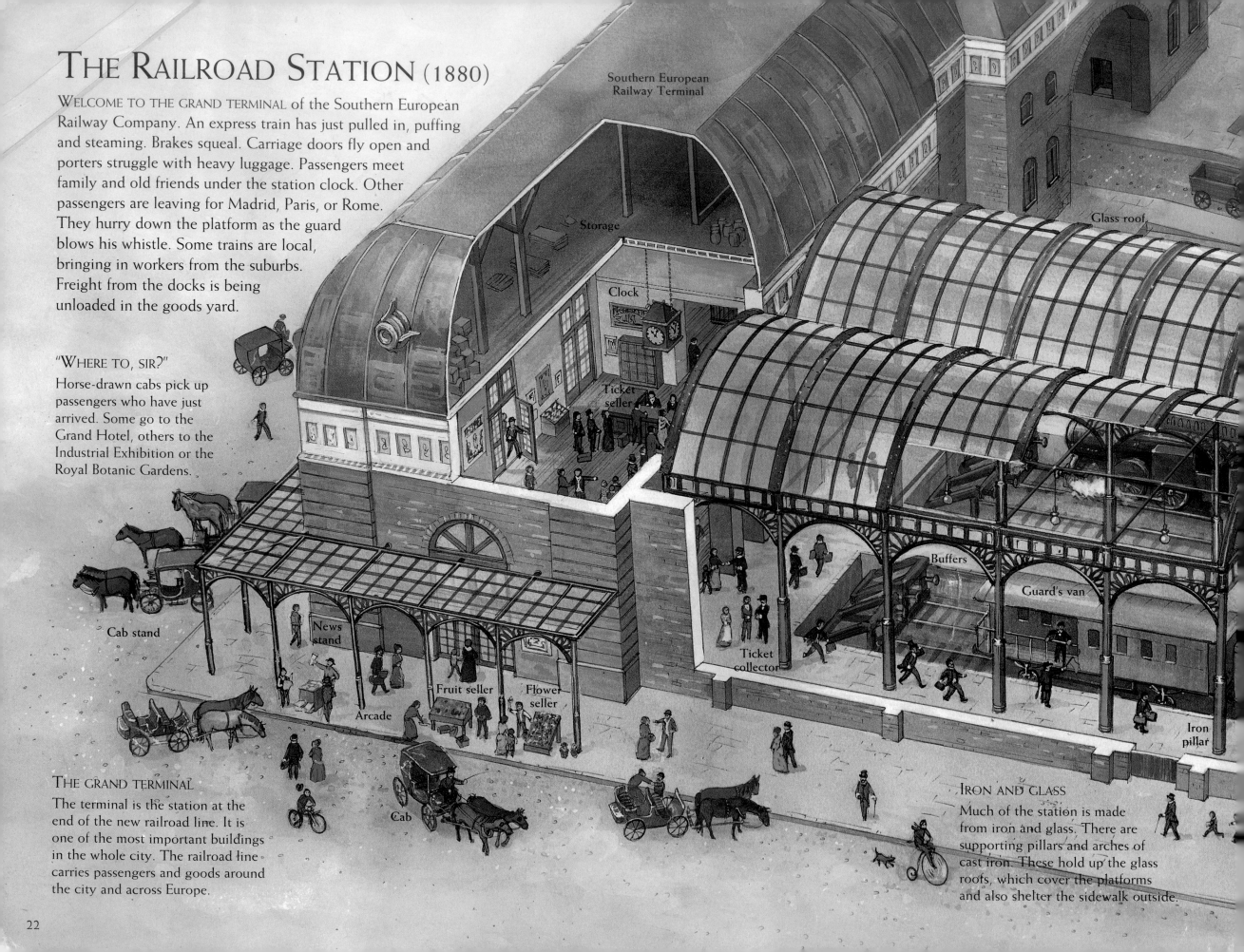

THE RAILROAD STATION (1880)

WELCOME TO THE GRAND TERMINAL of the Southern European Railway Company. An express train has just pulled in, puffing and steaming. Brakes squeal. Carriage doors fly open and porters struggle with heavy luggage. Passengers meet family and old friends under the station clock. Other passengers are leaving for Madrid, Paris, or Rome. They hurry down the platform as the guard blows his whistle. Some trains are local, bringing in workers from the suburbs. Freight from the docks is being unloaded in the goods yard.

"WHERE TO, SIR?"
Horse-drawn cabs pick up passengers who have just arrived. Some go to the Grand Hotel, others to the Industrial Exhibition or the Royal Botanic Gardens.

Southern European Railway Terminal

Storage

Glass roof

Clock

Ticket seller

Buffers

Guard's van

Ticket collector

Cab stand

News stand

Fruit seller

Flower seller

Arcade

Iron pillar

THE GRAND TERMINAL
The terminal is the station at the end of the new railroad line. It is one of the most important buildings in the whole city. The railroad line carries passengers and goods around the city and across Europe.

Cab

IRON AND GLASS
Much of the station is made from iron and glass. There are supporting pillars and arches of cast iron. These hold up the glass roofs, which cover the platforms and also shelter the sidewalk outside.

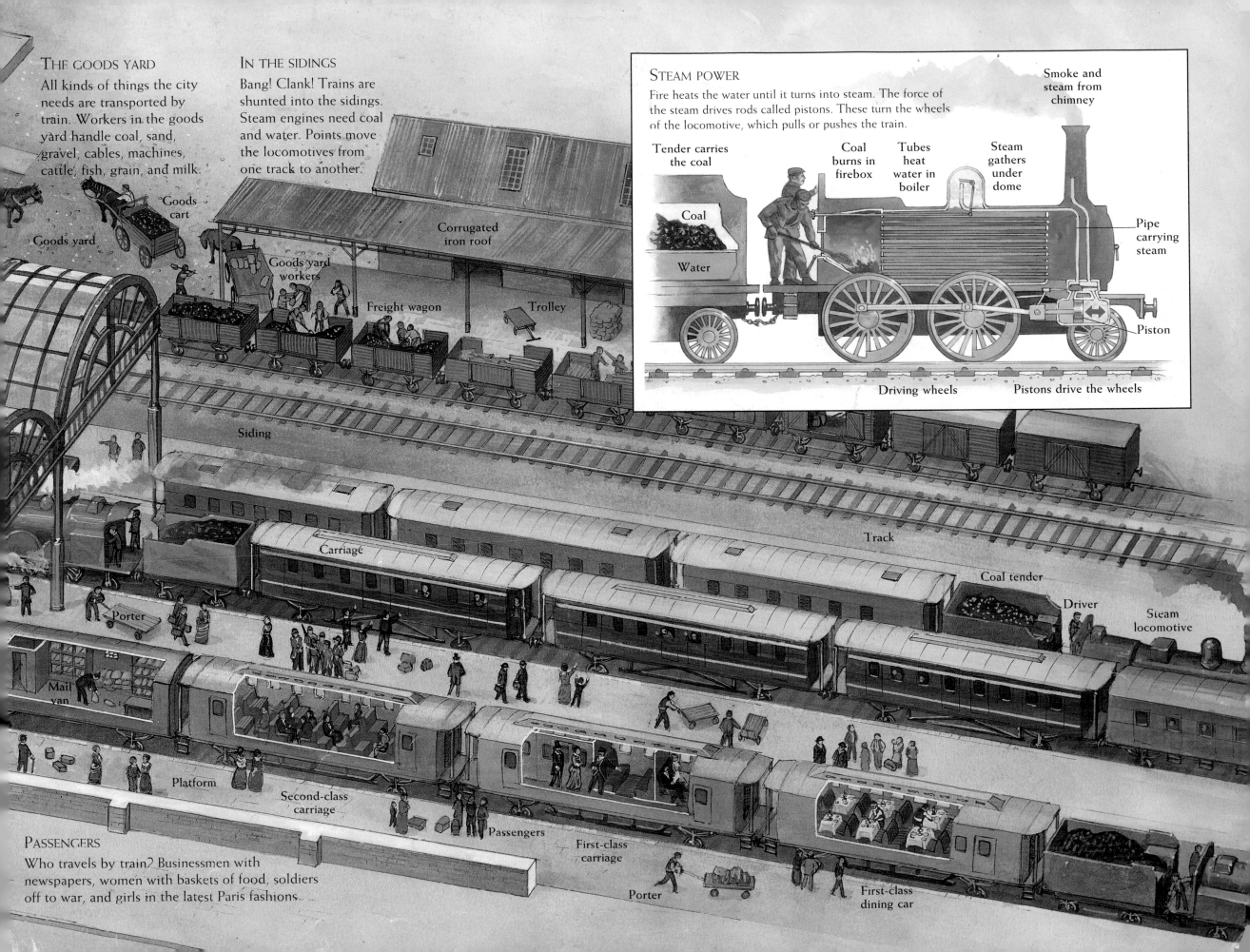

THE GOODS YARD

All kinds of things the city needs are transported by train. Workers in the goods yard handle coal, sand, gravel, cables, machines, cattle, fish, grain, and milk.

IN THE SIDINGS

Bang! Clank! Trains are shunted into the sidings. Steam engines need coal and water. Points move the locomotives from one track to another.

Goods cart

Goods yard

Goods yard workers

Corrugated iron roof

Freight wagon

Trolley

Siding

STEAM POWER

Fire heats the water until it turns into steam. The force of the steam drives rods called pistons. These turn the wheels of the locomotive, which pulls or pushes the train.

Smoke and steam from chimney

Tender carries the coal

Coal burns in firebox

Tubes heat water in boiler

Steam gathers under dome

Coal

Water

Pipe carrying steam

Piston

Driving wheels

Pistons drive the wheels

Track

Carriage

Coal tender

Driver

Steam locomotive

Porter

Mail van

Platform

Second-class carriage

Passengers

First-class carriage

First-class dining car

Porter

PASSENGERS

Who travels by train? Businessmen with newspapers, women with baskets of food, soldiers off to war, and girls in the latest Paris fashions.

STEEL AND GLASS (2005)

THE STREETS LIGHT UP as it gets dark. There are car headlights, traffic lights, glowing store signs, and flashing advertisements. Office workers switch off their computers and hurry home. People crowd into subway stations, shopping malls, movie theaters, and parks. Everyone seems to be in a hurry. The Old Town on the hill is lit up as well. It is now just part of a huge, modern city.

TV mast

Railroad bridge

Hospital

Hotel

Apartment block

Gym

Swimming pool

Children's bedroom

Hairdresser's

Boardroom

Apartments

Shopping complex

Tow truck

Kitchen

Fashion

Office

Bathroom

Living room

Ambulance

Street sweeper

Electrical goods

Bus

Rooftop café

Shoes

Corner store

Crosswalk

Outdoor heater

Cash machine

Underground parking lot

Vending machines

Minivan

Haulage vehicle

Cell phone

Waiter

Laptop computer

Neon sign

Motorcycle courier

Traffic wardens

Businesswoman

Tourists

Phone booth

Taxi

WHO'S WHO?

Here are some of the people you might meet in the modern city.

 The **waiter** balances drinks on his tray and can carry several plates of hot food at once.

The **architect** designs new buildings. He has to know about modern building materials.

 The **street musician** sings songs to passers-by. If they like his music, they throw coins into his hat.

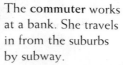 The **commuter** works at a bank. She travels in from the suburbs by subway.

The **construction worker** wears a hard hat on the building site.

 The **motorcycle courier** darts through the traffic, delivering packages from one office to another.

Sports stadium

Movie theater

Old Town

Financial district

Millennium Tower

Railroad station

Theater

Museum

College

Advertising screen

Shopping mall

Apartment block

Escalators

Pedestrian zone

Solar panels

Pedestrian glass bridge

Café

Tourist boat

Billboard

Monument

Tennis court

Articulated bus

Bus shelter

Marina

Street light

Wharfs

Traffic lights

Cyclist

Jogger

Underground train tunnel under the riverbed

Refrigerated truck

TV crew

Delivery van

Craft stalls

Fast-food vendor

Mailbox

Subway

School trip

Rollerblader

Graffiti

Skateboarder

 The **gym instructor** helps office workers get in shape. They visit the gym after work to do exercises.

 The **paramedic** travels in an ambulance. She is trained to save lives if there is a bad accident.

 This **policewoman** controls the traffic. She tries to keep the cars moving, preventing traffic jams.

 The **street sweeper** picks up trash, such as soft-drink cans, candy wrappers, and carry-out food cartons.

 This **tourist** is lining up to take a boat trip along the river. She plans to take some photographs of the castle ruins.

 The mayor of the city is making a speech. She talks of her plans for the city's future.

25

HIGH-RISE (2005)

THE MILLENNIUM TOWER was built in the year 2000. Its strong foundations of steel and concrete are pinned into the ancient bedrock beneath the city. This tall building contains offices, stores, a hotel, a movie theater, and a gymnasium—it is like a city in miniature. Take an elevator to the rooftop restaurant, and the whole city is spread out below. Look to the north and you can see the Old City district, where the story of the city began.

SAVING ENERGY

This is a smart building, designed to save energy. Insulation, such as double-glazed windows and living tiles of green grass on the roof, prevents heat from being lost. Solar panels collect energy from the Sun. They trap the heat and use it to warm water supplies.

SCRAPING THE SKY

A high-rise, or skyscraper, has many floors. Only a few of them are shown here.

DINING IN THE SKY

The rooftop restaurant has one of the best views in the entire city. It serves the seafood and wine for which the region is famous.

WORKING OUT

Busy office workers, who spend all day sitting at a computer, come to the gymnasium on the ninth floor to get fit. There are all kinds of exercise machines.

OFFICES

At the advertising company, people think up ways to sell cars, CDs, and all kinds of other products. Their advertisements appear on television and in magazines.

BEATING THE HEAT

Air-conditioning vents run between floors and lead to and from each room. They make sure that the air inside the building is neither too hot nor too cold, and neither too dry nor too dusty.

GOING UP!

High-rises depend on elevators. The Millennium Tower has an express elevator that whizzes up the outside of the building to the restaurant. The main elevators are on the inside of the building.

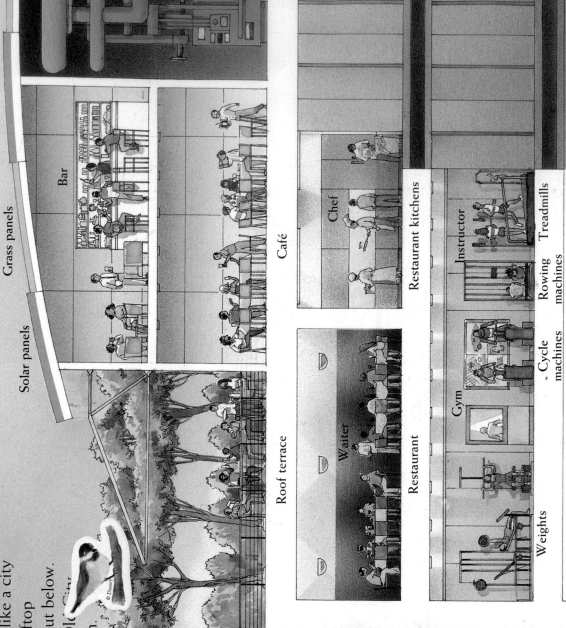

Solar panels

Grass panels

Bar

Café

Chef

Roof terrace

Waiter

Restaurant

Restaurant kitchens

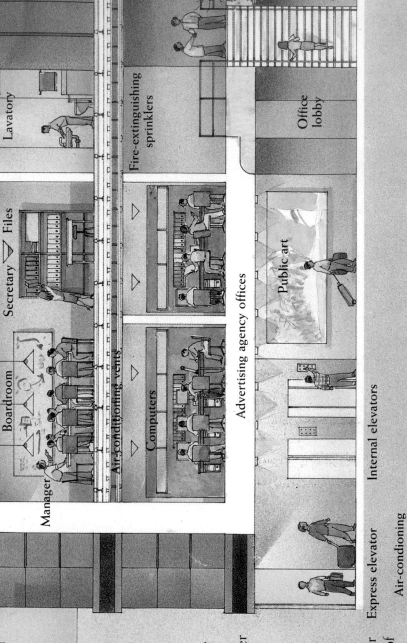

Instructor

Gym

Cycle machines

Rowing machines

Treadmills

Weights

Boardroom

Manager

Secretary

Files

Computers

Air-conditioning vents

Advertising agency offices

Lavatory

Fire-extinguishing sprinklers

Public art

Office lobby

Office reception

Express elevator   Internal elevators

Air-condioning external vents

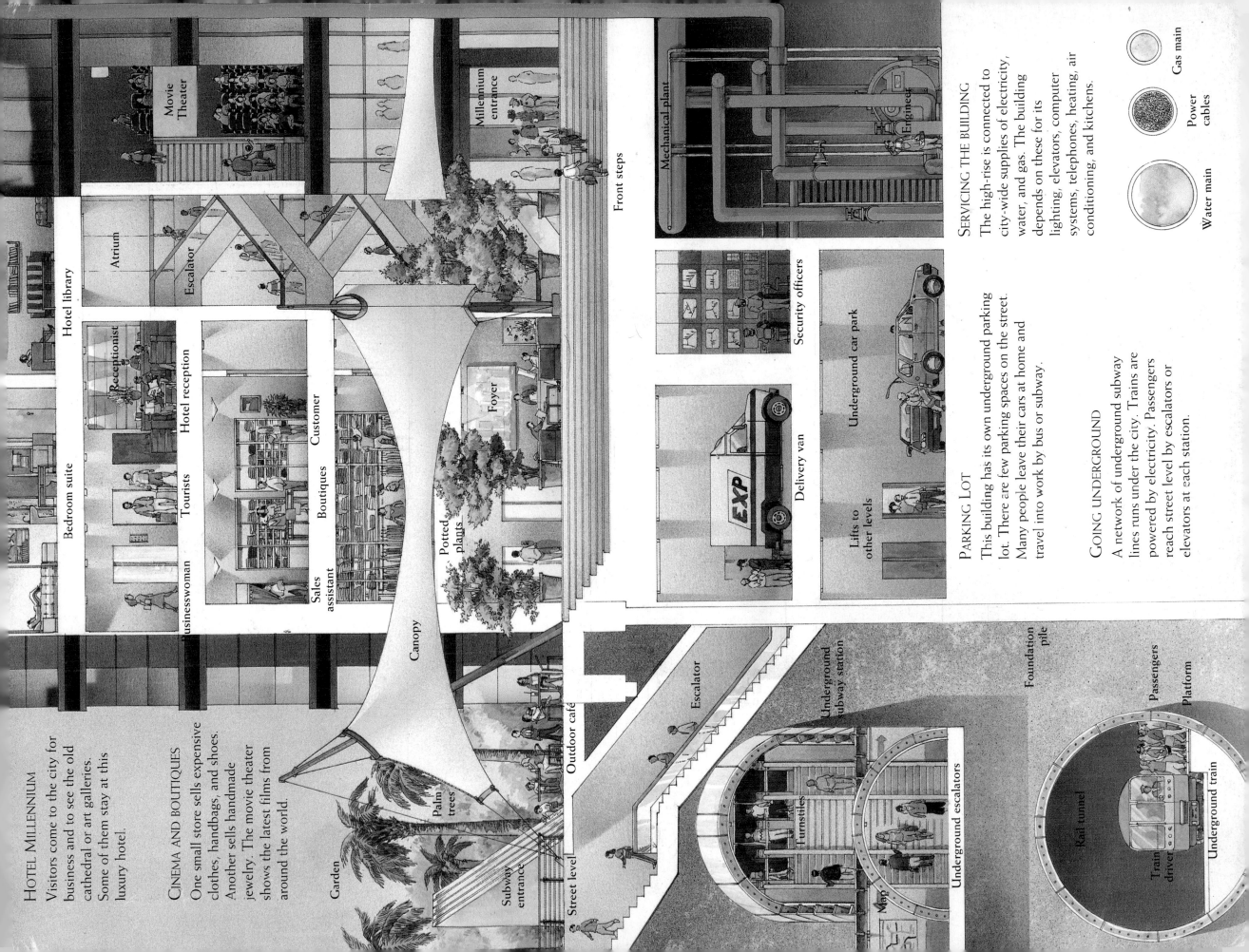

HOTEL MILLENNIUM

Visitors come to the city for business and to see the old cathedral or art galleries. Some of them stay at this luxury hotel.

CINEMA AND BOUTIQUES

One small store sells expensive clothes, handbags, and shoes. Another sells handmade jewelry. The movie theater shows the latest films from around the world.

SERVICING THE BUILDING

The high-rise is connected to city-wide supplies of electricity, water, and gas. The building depends on these for its lighting, elevators, computer systems, telephones, heating, air conditioning, and kitchens.

PARKING LOT

This building has its own underground parking lot. There are few parking spaces on the street. Many people leave their cars at home and travel into work by bus or subway.

GOING UNDERGROUND

A network of underground subway lines runs under the city. Trains are powered by electricity. Passengers reach street level by escalators or elevators at each station.

GLOSSARY: ARCHITECTURE

GREEK

Acropolis: A rocky area of high ground at the center of most Greek cities. It was easy to defend and was often the site of forts and temples.

Agora: The city center, made up of a busy marketplace and public buildings.

Colony: A settlement built in another land. The Greeks built colonies throughout their history.

Column: A stone pillar designed to support a roof.

Gymnasium: An area for men and boys to exercise and play sports. It was also a place for meeting and discussion.

Pediment: A triangular gable or roof end, often decorated with painted sculptures.

Stoa: A building with columns and walkways, used as a meeting place.

Theater: An open-air arena with rows of stone benches, arranged in a half-circle and set into a hillside. Greek drama was performed here.

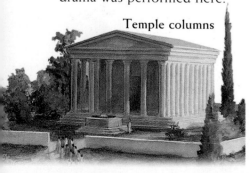
Temple columns

ROMAN

Amphitheater: An oval or circular building with seats for spectators. In the center was an arena (area of sand), where shows were staged.

Arches and domes: Strong curved structures that support themselves. Engineers used them in buildings and bridges.

Cloacae: Drains and sewers built in many towns to carry waste and dirty water into the nearest river.

Inside an amphitheater

Domus: A house, often designed around an open atrium (courtyard).

Forum: An open square at the center of a Roman town. It was a public meeting place and was surrounded by shops, temples, and public buildings.

Insula: An "island" or block of housing within the streets of a Roman town. In large cities, it might be taken up by a tall, crowded apartment block.

Villa: A large, grand home built outside the town by a wealthy Roman.

MEDIEVAL

Battlements: The upper walls of a castle or city defenses. They were used as a platform for fighting and as a shield.

Cathedral: The most important Christian church in a region, and often the largest and most splendid.

Crenels: Gaps in battlement walls. Arrows could be fired through the crenels, or rocks could be dropped onto the enemy below.

City walls: Thick stone walls surrounded the whole city during in medieval times. They were used to defend the city from attack. The gates were closed at night.

Loops: Narrow slits in castle and city walls, used for firing arrows at the enemy.

Merlons: Raised sections of battlements. They provided cover from attack.

Monastery: A building where monks lived and worshipped. Many medieval monasteries also served as libraries, schools, or hospitals.

Medieval cathedral

17TH CENTURY

Coats-of-arms: Badges used by noble families since medieval times. Coats-of-arms of families, guilds of traders and craftspeople, and cities were often carved into stone walls or displayed on flags, banners, and tapestries.

Palace and garden

Gardens: In the 1600s, gardens were laid out around palaces, public buildings, and squares. They included low hedges and paths arranged in intricate patterns, as well as statues and fountains.

Inn: A building that offered food, drink, and a bed for people, and stabling for horses. Inns were also places to rent horses or to start a journey by horse-drawn coach.

Palace: A grand house with many rooms, built for noble or royal families. It was not fortified against attack.

Theater: An enclosed public building for performances. Plays took place on a stage in front of painted scenery. Theaters might be closed during times of plague, or if the king did not like the play.

19TH CENTURY

Botanical gardens: Gardens whose gardeners collected plants for scientific study. Their new greenhouses, like railroad station roofs, were made of cast iron and glass.

Factories: Large, brick buildings with tall, smoking chimneys. Factories and mills contained machinery that produced steel, glass, cloth, and pottery on a large scale.

Hospitals: New hospitals were were light and airy. Doctors and nurses learned to keep wards clean and free of germs.

Prisons: New prisons were built with cells and high walls. They were cleaner and less damp than dungeons.

Schools: For the first time, all children got the chance of a basic education. Schools were built in many European cities.

Sewers: Brick tunnels for carrying sewage, built under streets to replace open drains.

Suspension bridge: A bridge whose roadway is supported by hanging chains or cables.

Suspension bridge

MODERN

Telecommunication masts: Antennas, some on top of high buildings, used to relay radio, television, and phone signals.

Escalators: Moving staircases in large stores, shopping malls, airports, and underground subways.

Lifts: Transport people up and down tall buildings. Lifts were essential for the development of skyscrapers.

High-rise buildings: Tall buildings built around steel frames. Their foundations are embedded deep in rock.

Shopping mall

Pedestrian zone: An area in a city centre with streets given over to walkers, not cars.

Shopping mall: A building where people can visit many shops at different levels.

Underground car park: A place to leave cars below street level, built to create more space in crowded cities.

TECHNOLOGY

GREEK

Coins: Greeks were making coins and trading with them from 595 BC. A smith placed a disk of hot metal on a raised metal pattern called a die. He then hammered the disk to create a patterned coin.

Metalwork: Greeks made bronze from about 2900 BC and still use it for armor and helmets. They used iron from about 1050 BC, to make swords, spears, ax-heads, knives, and hammers.

Pottery: The Greeks shaped clay pots on a wheel and heated them in an oven at about 1,000°F (540°C). They often painted scenes on the pots of gods and goddesses, or of everyday life.

Transportation: The wealthy used horses for travel. The poor used donkeys and mules. Oxen hauled wagons. Fast chariots were used for racing, but no longer for battles.

Triremes: Greek warships made of wood, with a crew of 200. They were powered by three banks of oars on each side.

Greek metalworkers

ROMAN

Aqueduct: A stone channel or pipe, used to carry water.

Cement: Substance made of lime and sand, used since 300 BC as a kind of glue for binding together stonework.

Concrete: A mixture of lime and ground rock, invented in around 55 BC. It was cheaper and often stronger than stone.

Roman aqueduct

Iron: The most important metal for the Romans. Smiths hammered out tools, weapons, armor, pots, and pans.

Glass: The Romans were great glassmakers. They knew how to blow hot glass into shapes through a long tube, and made bottles, bowls, and pitchers.

Pottery: The Romans had large pottery factories wherever there were good supplies of clay. There were big centers of production in Italy, France, and Germany.

Roads: The Romans built a road system across Europe. The roads were straight, well drained, and built on strong foundations. They were paved with stone slabs, gravel, or stone chippings.

MEDIEVAL

Candles: Candles made from animal fat had been used for lighting since Greek times. In medieval times, fine candles were made from beeswax. Some were marked in stages to show the time they took to burn. These candles were an early sort of clock.

Milling: The flour for the city's bakers was produced by grinding grain between great, millstones. In windmills, the wind power was used to turn millstones. In watermills, flowing water powered a waterwheel, which provided the turning power. Mills were also used to press olives and to crush seeds to make oil.

Shipping: European merchant ships were small and clumsy, with square sails. They traded mostly in coastal waters. Later, Europeans adopted rudders and triangular sails from the Arabs and Chinese. Then they could make great ocean voyages.

Tiles: In southern Europe, roofs were made of pottery tiles. They were less of a fire hazard than the thatched roofs of Northern Europe.

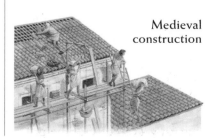

Medieval construction

17TH CENTURY

Muskets: Guns that needed to be rested on a support to be fired. They took a long time to load. The gunpowder was set off by a shower of sparks.

Scientist with a telescope

Lenses: Curved pieces of glass that were made for microscopes, which made small objects look bigger, and telescopes, which made distant objects look nearer.

Springs: Well-made metal springs had an impact on the way devices were made in the 1600s. Small springs were used in making better clocks and guns. Big metal springs were used in building horse-drawn coaches. The springs cushioned passengers against bumps in the road.

Weather instruments: New instruments were invented to measure different kinds of weather. The thermometer measured temperature and the barometer measured air pressure. When air pressure is high, the weather is fine. Barometers helped people forecast the weather. The first weather stations kept daily records from the 1650s.

19TH CENTURY

Aircraft: Balloons carried the first air passengers in the 1780s. The first powered airships were flown in 1852.

Bicycles: The first bicycle was built in 1839. Air-filled rubber tires appeared in 1888.

Cars: Gas-driven cars were invented in Germany in 1885. Within 30 years, new streets and roads were built, traffic lights and speed limits were introduced, and exhaust fumes polluted the air.

Steamships: Iron ships driven by propellers date from 1843. Steamships allowed reliable, fast travel across the ocean.

Street lighting: Gas street lights appeared in Europe in 1814. The first street with permanent electric lighting was in the French city of Lyon, in 1857.

Telephones: Exchanges were opening in European cities by 1879, changing the way people did business and enjoyed themselves.

Steam car

MODERN

CCTV: Closed-circuit television (CCTV) cameras operate in city centers. They record traffic movements and any crimes or accidents that may occur on the streets.

Cellular telephones: The first service started in the US in 1984. Since the 1990s, cell phones have changed the way people communicate with friends, families, and the people they work with.

Traffic jam

Computers: Offices began to use big computers in the 1950s. The first personal computers appeared in 1975. The international computer network known as the Internet began in 1987.

Plastics: Cheap, light, artificial materials that can be molded into any shape. They are used to make packaging, clothing, eyeglasses, furniture, and countless everyday objects.

Prestressed concrete: Used in skyscrapers, bridges, and flyovers, this material is set around tense steel wires for extra strength.

WORK AND PLAY

GREEK

Drama: The first Greek plays were performed as part of religious festivals. Only men were allowed to act. They wore masks that showed characters or feelings.

Games: Athletics contests held in honor of the gods. Events included running, wrestling, throwing the discus, and chariot racing. Winners received prizes and glory in their hometown.

Philosophy: Philosophers tried to answer questions about the world in a scientific way. Later, they discussed questions of right and wrong.

Politics: The study and practice of government. The word comes from the Greek for city, "polis." Some cities were ruled by kings, some by assemblies of citizens.

Slavery: Greek society relied on slaves to do the hard work without pay.

Warfare: Male citizens served in the army for part of the year and during wartime.

Slaves serving at a banquet

ROMAN

Army: The army was organized into 28 legions, which were groups of 5,500 professional soldiers. The soldiers had to be Roman citizens.

Boardgames: The Romans liked to play boardgames and to gamble with dice.

Exercising at the public baths

Bread supply: Cities imported grain each year to feed their citizens. Donkeys turned millstones, which ground the grain into flour. Loaves were baked in big ovens and some were given to poor people at public expense.

Chariot racing: Four horses normally pulled each chariot. Winners could make a fortune in prize money.

Farming: Many retired soldiers owned small farms outside the city walls. Most farms had vegetable plots, fruit trees, and beehives. Richer people owned country estates with larger farms and orchards.

Medicine: Roman doctors knew little science. However, some of their herbal potions worked, and surgeons knew how to set bones.

MEDIEVAL

Knights: Horseback soldiers who became powerful in the Middle Ages. They took oaths of loyalty to a lord and had to serve him when called upon. They were supposed to follow a code of honor.

Pilgrimage: A journey to a sacred place made for religious reasons. Pilgrims traveled across Europe to pray at famous shrines or churches. They wore badges to show where they had been.

Players: Traveling actors who performed plays from wagons or on the steps of cathedrals. The plays were about the lives of saints or events in the Bible. They featured comic scenes and special effects.

Troubadours: Poets and musicians in southern Europe who wandered from castle to castle. They would praise the local ruler and sing of love.

Weight masters: Officials who watched market traders to make sure they did not cheat by selling underweight goods.

Traveling players

17TH CENTURY

Actresses: Women could now act on stage in many countries. They became popular, like today's pop stars.

Courtiers: Nobles who spent post of their time in the royal court. They hoped to gain favors from the king.

Guards: Men with muskets or pikes who formed companies to protect important people or to keep order in cities.

Printing press

Printing: Printing presses were now common in Europe. They replaced scribes who copied books by hand. Presses turned out pamphlets and books. If they criticized the king or the church, the printer was thrown into jail.

Science: Scientists studied the stars. Doctors discovered how the human body works. Some science was still mixed up with superstition. Alchemists tried to find out how to make gold and how to live forever.

Tax collectors: Officials told by the king to collect taxes. They often took much of the money for themselves and became very wealthy.

19TH CENTURY

Bargees: Men who sailed barges along the rivers and canals of Europe. Barges were like the trucks of their day, transporting industrial goods.

Factory workers: People poured into cities in search of work in factories. Work was poorly paid, dangerous, and unhealthy. Many campaigned for better working conditions.

Industrialists: Factory owners who gambled by buying and selling shares in companies. Some became so rich that they never had to work.

Lamp lighting: Gas lamps in city streets had to be lit one by one at nightfall.

Popular songs: Songs that became well known through music halls, opera houses, and dance halls. Families sang them at home, at the piano.

Sports: Cycling, rowing, lawn tennis, gymnastics, archery, soccer, boxing, and billiards all became popular across Europe during this period.

Opera house

MODERN

Jogging: Many people like to go for a jog in the park before they go to work, or at lunchtime. It keeps them fit.

Road transportation: Trucks take goods across Europe by road. The containers on the back are all the same size, so they can stack neatly.

Office workers: Workers who sit at desks, use computers and calculators, and talk to clients on the telephone.

Rooftop restaurant

Sports stadium: Thousands of people gather at stadiums to watch sports. Some of the biggest are built for the Olympic Games, which are held every four years.

Television: Most homes have televisions, which pick up programs by antenna, satellite dish, or cable. Televisions show news, game shows, drama, music, and sports.

Traffic wardens: If you park in the wrong place, a traffic warden may give you a parking ticket. You may have to pay a fine, or have your car clamped or towed away.

Costume

Greek

Armor: Soldiers shielded their head and cheeks with crested bronze helmets. They wore a solid bronze cuirass—a combined back- and breast-plate. Bronze greaves (shin guards) protected their legs.

Chiton: A long linen tunic worn by men and women. It was joined over the shoulders and so needed no fastenings.

Hairstyles: Women wore their hair long, often in ringlets. Some tied their hair with nets or ribbons. Men wore their hair short and curled.

Headwear: Some women covered their heads with veils or cloaks. Men went bare-headed, but sometimes wore pointed woolen caps or straw sunhats with big brims.

Peplos: A woman's long woolen dress. It was gathered at the waist and fastened at the shoulder with brooches.

Sandals: Both women and men wore sandals made of leather thongs. Men sometimes wore boots.

Greek soldiers in bronze armor

Roman

Armor: Soldiers wore upper body armor of overlapping bronze plates, which were strapped together, or a mail shirt of interlaced iron rings.

Armor   Toga

Cosmetics: Women liked to wear makeup. Powder was made from chalk and eye-shadow from ash. Lipstick was made from red ocher (clay) or wine dregs.

Palla: A long shawl worn by women and draped around the head and shoulders.

Stola: A long dress worn by women over an undertunic.

Toga: A white robe of heavy wool. It was the formal wear of important men. The togas of the most important men had a purple border.

Working dress: Workers and slaves wore simple woolen or linen tunics, which allowed them to move freely.

Wreath: A crown of laurel leaves worn on the head of emperors, successful athletes at the games, and soldiers honored for their bravery.

Medieval

Armor: knights wore tunics and leggings made of chain mail. Soon knights began to strap metal plates over their mail for extra protection. On top, they wore a light tunic called a surcoat.

Crowns: Kings wore crowns as badges of royalty. Other royal symbols included rings, gloves, cloaks, swords, and staffs called scepters.

Hose: linen or wool leg coverings, rather like tights. They were tucked into pointed boots or shoes of soft leather.

Religious dress: Priests wore long robes. Bishops wore pointed hats called miters. Monks shaved their heads. Each order of monks had its own dress, or habit.

Knights in armor and surcoats

Tunic: A loose, sleeveless top, usually reaching the knees or the midthighs. In the year 1250, both men and women's dress was based upon a tunic design. Noblemen, merchants, and lawyers wore a long costume, while working men wore a short costume, which was more practical.

17th Century

Breeches: Short pants fastened just below the knee. They were fashionable for men from about 1520 until full-length pants became more popular during the 1800s.

Children's dress: Babies were tightly bound in bands called swaddling clothes until they were 6 weeks old. Boys and girls then wore pinafores (long dresses). Boys started to wear breeches at 6 years old.

17th-century fashion

Fans: In southern Europe, fashionable ladies carried beautiful fans made of silk or ivory to keep themselves cool in the heat of summer.

Military dress: Most soldiers wore only a breastplate and helmet over their normal clothes. Uniforms were beginning to be worn by the 1660s and 70s.

Petticoats: In the early 1600s, full skirts were draped over hoops worn around a woman's waist. In the 1650s, these were replaced by stiff petticoats.

Wigs: In the late 1600s, men and women took to wearing curled wigs, even if their hair was still in good condition.

19th Century

Cotton: A material imported to Europe in the 1800s and woven into cloth at large, industrial textile mills.

Dresses: Crinolines (full-skirted women's petticoats) were in fashion in the 1850s. In the 1880s, women wore narrower skirts with a bustle (a pad or frame inside the skirt) at the bottom.

Footwear: Shoes and ankle-length and knee-length boots were made of polished leather with buttons as fasteners.

Hats: Men wore top hats (tall black hats with a narrow brim). Women wore bonnets decorated with ribbons.

Pants: In the 1800s, men began to wear pants rather than breeches and stockings.

Uniforms: Soldiers wore neat uniforms in bright colors. Police forces wore uniforms, as did firemen, nurses, schoolchildren, and orphans.

Waterproofs: Waterproof clothes were made from cloth and rubber in the 1830s. The inventor's name, Macintosh, was given to all raincoats.

Dressed for a stroll

Modern

Jeans: Heavy cotton pants that were first made for workers in the US in the 1870s. They are now worn by ordinary men and women around the world. The name "jeans" comes from the Italian city of Genoa, which produced the cloth.

Modern dress

Sportswear: Special fibers and clothes are worn for many sports. Some are worn every day, such as sneakers, baseball hats, or soccer jerseys.

Suit: A matching jacket and pants for men or a matching jacket and skirt or pants for women. It is formal wear for business, and men wear it with a shirt and tie, and women usually wear it with a blouse.

Sunglasses: Dark glasses were invented in 1885 and remain fashionable today.

Synthetic fibers: Clothing is now often made of artificial fibers, such as nylon or Lycra®.

T-shirts: Cotton shirts with short sleeves worn by men and women. Many are printed with designs or slogans.

Time-traveling quiz

Can you find these characters and objects from the past and present city? Search through the pages of this book and find out when they were there.

These women are cutting stalks of wheat with a sickle made of flint. They are **farming**.

These children have to learn things by heart. If they make a mistake they are beaten with a stick by their **tutor**.

This figure is not a human being, but a god of the sea!. If you are sailor you might say a prayer to him. His name is **Poseidon**.

Stepping stones help people cross the street of a Roman city when the street is full of puddles, mud, or garbage.

How do you clean away the city grime without any soap? You could use oil and a **strigil** (a scraper).

This carriage looks very grand, but it must be bumpy to ride in. It belongs to the **countess**.

These **nobles** are visiting a castle. The count has asked them to attend a banquet.

These **merchants** have arrived by ship from North Africa. They are trading in cloths and spices.

This **portrait** still hangs in the town hall today. When do you think it was painted?

Can you find a man with his head under a cloth? He's a **photographer** using an old-fashioned camera.

You must show the **ticket collector** that you have the right ticket when you get on the train.

Somewhere, there is a **skateboarder** flying along the sidewalk. This could be you, now!

Can you find this street? At its end, on the distant hill, can you make out the remains of the **Old Town**? They are a record of the long history of the city.

Index

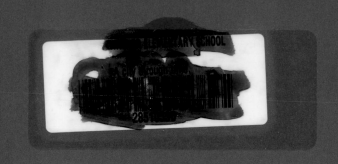

Steele, Philip.

A city through time.

$17.99   28510530

DATE			

BAKER & TAYLOR